GRAMMAR CAN BE FUN

Words
and
Pictures

By
MUNRO
LEAF

A STOKES BOOK

J. B. LIPPINCOTT COMPANY

PHILADELPHIA

NEW YORK

Twenty-first Impression

Under Government regulations for saving paper
during the war, the thickness of this book has
been reduced below the customary peacetime
standards. The text is complete and unabridged.

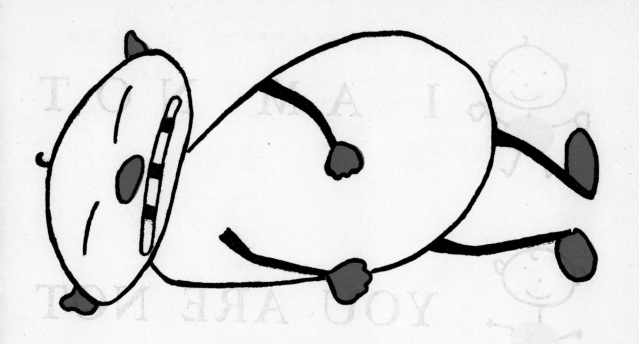

THIS IS AIN'T

Now you see why no one even likes to hear his name.

Never say AIN'T.

That is being just as lazy as he is.

Say—

3

 I AM NOT

 YOU ARE NOT

 HE or  SHE IS NOT

 THEY ARE NOT

4

THE WOBBLY NECKS

UH-HUH   UN-UN

Poor Wobbly Necks! They shake their heads and nod their heads and still no one knows what they want to say.

Some one says, "Would you like to go?" and they shout

UH-HUH and UN-UN

then

Wiggle and Wiggle and Wiggle.

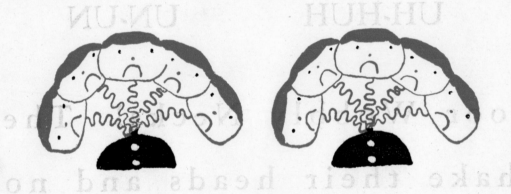

But no one knows
what they mean.

While——

YES and NO
Are always happy.

Everybody knows

what THEY mean

and

THEY don't have to

wiggle their

necks

at

all.

And this is one of the
most awful little
creatures of all.

YEAH

PLEASE LET'S NEVER

HEAR HIM AGAIN!

This is
GIMME

Doesn't he look like a spider?

All day long he shouts
GIMME this, GIMME that
and grabs with all those hands.
If he should say

PLEASE GIVE ME

he would be much nicer and
he wouldn't look so queer.

GIMME has two little sisters
who are just as bad as he is.

They are

GONNA   and   WANNA

GONNA just   WANNA just
will not say   will not say
what she should,   what she should,
which is   which is

GOING TO   WANT TO

Don't YOU be
like

GONNA   GIMME   or   WANNA

 Poor Old G **G**

Don't you feel sorry for poor old G? He gets so lonely.

So many children leave him out when they talk about things that are fun—like

PLAYIN—

DANCIN—

RUNNIN—

FISHIN—

WHERE IS

POOR G

?

Let's always take 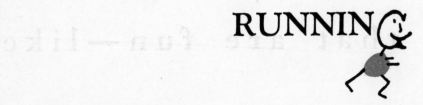 along too.

PLAYIN •

DANCIN

RUNNIN

and

FISHIN

He has such a good time!

This is CAN

CAN

He is able to do things.
That means he is old
enough, or big enough, or
strong enough to do them.

This is MAY

She is polite and
asks when she wants
to do things.

MAY

You would not say

Mother, CAN I have an apple?

Everybody knows that you are old enough, and big enough, and strong enough to have an apple.

You mean to say

Mother, MAY I have an apple?

and

I

will

tell

you

a

secret.

If you say PLEASE when you say MAY , you will probably get what you want more quickly.

LY (say it LEE)

This is LY the China Boy

who likes action and movement of any kind.

If you walk or run, dance or sing, all of those take action.

That is doing things and that is what LY likes.

So he comes along.

I walk slowLY <u>not</u> slow.

I run quickLY <u>not</u> quick.

I dance lightLY  <u>not</u> light.

I sing loudLY <u>not</u> loud.

This is all about a very
messy creature and her
name is GOT.

Here she is.

And I'll tell you what she is.
She is a weed that grows
in sentences, if you don't
take care of them.

Good sentences are like good gardens.

There is plenty of room for the words that belong there like

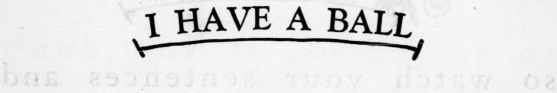

I HAVE A BALL

But——

When a messy word like

 grows there, everything

is jumbled.

In sentences

and
in gardens

so watch your sentences and

keep away.

This  is NOT

Sometimes people say NOT

so quickly it is just N'T

like haveN'T

This  is NO

They are both nice, but

they should not get

together in the same

sentence.

They push and shove each

other—

just as they would if

they tried to sit in

the same chair.

This way.

I do NOT have NO books.

I doN'T want NO apple.

But——

If you let each one have

a sentence of his own,

it is fine, and they are

both happy.

I have NO books.

I doN'T want an apple.

NOW
We shall go very

slowLY.

Everybody can DO THINGS

and

Everybody can HAVE THINGS

DONE TO HIM.

Now

When we DO THINGS
we are called

I   **HE**   **SHE**   **THEY**

this way

I  hit the ball.

HE hit the ball.

SHE hit the ball.

That is DOING THINGS.

When we HAVE THINGS
DONE TO US
we are called

ME   **HIM**   **HER**   **THEM**

this way

The ball hit ME.

The ball hit HIM.

The ball hit HER.

That is HAVING THINGS
DONE TO US.

Now think of us this way—
Are we DOING THINGS, or are
we HAVING THINGS DONE TO US?

and

you will always know which

we are called.

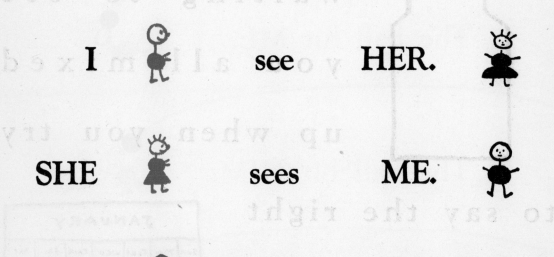

I   see   HER.

SHE   sees   ME.

HE   chased   THEM.

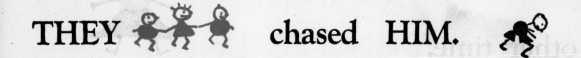

THEY   chased   HIM.

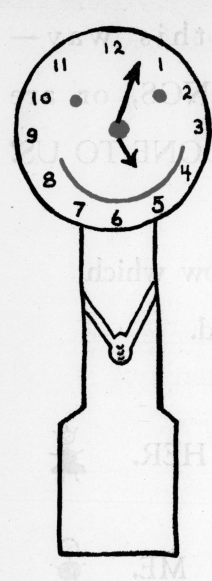

Do you know why old Mr. Clock and Mrs. Calendar are laughing so?

They are just waiting to see you all mixed up when you try to say the right word for what happened at some

other time.

You say now I SING.

That is easy.

But

If you did it yesterday,

WHAT do you say

And if you have finished

singing—WHAT do you

say

You should say

Now I SING.

 Some time ago

I SANG.

And if you have finished,

you say

I HAVE SUNG.

When I am thirsty

   I DRINK WATER.

   Some time ago

   I DRANK WATER

and when I have finished

I HAVE DRUNK WATER.

If I am hungry

I EAT food.

 Some time ago

I ATE FOOD

and when I have finished

I HAVE EATEN food.

If I look out of the window

I SEE people.

 Some time ago

I SAW people

and when I have finished

I HAVE SEEN people.

In the morning

I GO to school.

 Some time ago

I WENT to school

and when I have finished

I HAVE GONE to school.

In school

I DO arithmetic.

 Some time ago

I DID arithmetic.

When I have finished

I HAVE DONE arithmetic.

DO is a word that mixes us up another way—that is, when we use it with NOT and say it quickly, DON'T.

We say

I DO NOT

or quickly I DON'T

and we say

YOU DO NOT

or quickly YOU DON'T.

But we say

HE SHE

or

DOES NOT.

Never, Never

HE or SHE DON'T.

When I am sleepy

I LIE in bed.

 Some time ago

I LAY in bed.

When I have finished

I HAVE LAIN in bed.

If I have read my book

I LAY it there.

 Some time ago

I LAID it there.

When I have finished

I HAVE LAID it there.

Do those two get you mixed?

Well, remember that

IF	**IF**
you stretch yourself out	you put something else somewhere

you **LIE** down.	you **LAY** it there.
Some time ago you **LAY** down.	Some time ago you **LAID** it there.
And when finished you **HAVE LAIN** down.	And when finished you **HAVE LAID** it there.

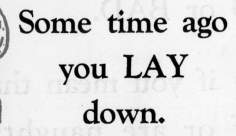

If someone says,  How do you feel?

You say

I feel WELL or ILL

not

I feel GOOD or BAD.

That is what you say if you mean that you behave yourself or are naughty.

And that is not what he wants to know.

THESE NEXT

PAGES HAVE

MISTAKES

I MAKE

AND

THE PICTURES

ARE DRAWN

BY